ŠEVČÍK

OPUS 2 PART 4

SCHOOL OF BOWING
TECHNIQUE

SCHULE DER
BOGENTECHNIK

ÉCOLE DU MÉCANISME
DE L'ARCHET

for
CELLO

ARR. FEUILLARD

BOSWORTH

The Works of OTAKAR ŠEVČÍK

VIOLIN

LITTLE SEVCIK, Elementary Tutor
SEVCIK SCALES & ARPEGGIOS
HOW TO PRACTISE SEVCIK'S MASTERWORKS
INTRODUCTION TO SEVCIK VIOLIN STUDIES
from Op. 1 (by K. W. Rokos)

For More Advanced Pupils

OP. 1. SCHOOL OF VIOLIN TECHNIQUE.
Part 1. Exercises in the 1st Position.
Part 2. Exercises in the 2nd-7th Positions.
Part 3. Exercises in Change of Position.
Part 4. Exercises in Double-Stopping, Triple-Stopping, Quadruple-Stopping (3 & 4-part chords). Pizzicato, Flageolet Tones, Harmonics.

OP. 1. Complete, bound in Cloth.

Development of the Right Hand

OP. 2. SCHOOL OF BOWING TECHNIQUE.
(4,000 Exercises in Bowing)
Parts 1-6
Exercise Themes to Op. 2.

OP. 3. 40 VARIATIONS
Piano Accompaniment (optional)

OPS. 2 & 3, Complete, bound in Cloth.

Development of the Left Hand

OP. 6. VIOLIN METHOD FOR BEGINNERS.
Parts 1-5. 1st Position.
Part 6.   Studies Preparatory to the various Positions.
Part 7.   5th Position and combining the various Positions.

OP. 6. Complete, bound in Cloth.

For Slightly Advanced Pupils

OP. 7. STUDIES PREPARATORY TO THE SHAKE & DEVELOPMENT IN DOUBLE-STOPPING.
Part 1. Exercises in the 1st Position.
Part 2. Exercises in the 2nd, 3rd, 4th, 5th & 6th Positions.

OP. 8. CHANGES OF POSITION & PREPARATORY SCALE STUDIES.
In Thirds, Sixths, Octaves, & Tenths.

OP. 9. PREPARATORY STUDIES IN DOUBLE-STOPPING.
In Thirds, Sixths, Octaves & Tenths.

OPS. 7, 8 & 9. Complete, bound in Cloth.

VIOLA

Arranged by Lionel Tertis

OP. 1. SCHOOL OF TECHNIQUE.
Part 1.   Exercises in the 1st Position.
Part 2.   Exercises in the 2nd-7th Positions.
Part 3/4. Exercises in Changes of Position & in Double, Triple & Quadruple Stopping, etc.

OP. 2. SCHOOL OF BOWING TECHNIQUE.
Parts 1, 2 & 3.

OP. 3. FORTY VARIATIONS (arr. Margaret Major)
Piano Accompaniment (optional)

OP. 8. CHANGES OF POSITION & PREPARATORY SCALE STUDIES.

OP. 9. PREPARATORY STUDIES IN DOUBLE-STOPPING
(arr. Alan Arnold)

CELLO

OP. 1. THUMB PLACING EXERCISES.
Part 1. 1st Position (arr. W. Schultz)

OP. 2. SCHOOL OF BOWING TECHNIQUE
(4,000 Exercises arr. Feuillard)
Parts 1-6.

OP. 3. 40 VARIATIONS (arr. Feuillard)
Piano Accompaniment (optional)

OP. 8. CHANGES OF POSITION & PREPARATORY SCALE STUDIES.
In Thirds, Sixths, Octaves & Tenths (arr. H. Boyd)

BOSWORTH

Exclusive distributors:
Hal Leonard, 7777 West Bluemound Road, Milwaukee, WI 53213 Email: info@halleonard.com
Hal Leonard Europe Limited, 42 Wigmore Street Maryleborne, London, WIU 2 RY Email: info@halleonardeurope.com
Hal Leonard Australia Pty. Ltd. 4 Lentara Court Cheltenham, Victoria, 9132 Australia Email: info@halleonard.com.au

Heft IV	Cahier IV	Section IV
Arpeggien auf zwei Saiten.	**Arpèges sur deux cordes.**	**Arpeggios on two strings.**
	Sešit IV.	*Тетрадь IV*
	Arpéžie na dvou strunách.	**Арпеджіи на двухъ струнахъ.**

№ 31.

Etude in 17 Varianten mit Strich-arten zu jeder Veränderung.	Etude en 17 variantes avec les coups d'archet pour toutes les variantes.	Study in 17 Variations with the bowing-styles for each variation.
	Cvičení o 17 proměnách s případnými smyky ku každé proměně.	Этюдъ въ 17 варіантахъ съ движенія-ми смычка къ каждому варіанту.

Edited and translated by H. Brett.   Edited by L. R. Feuillard and A. E. Bosworth.

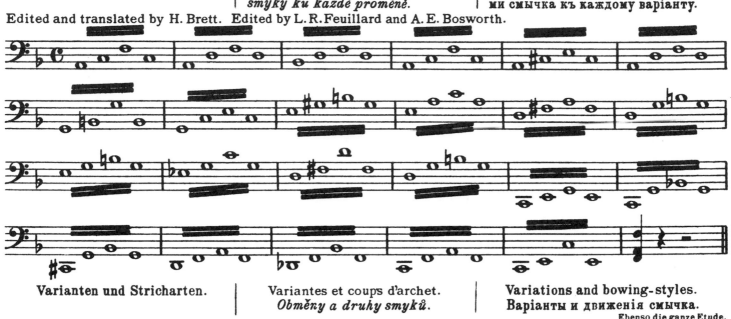

Varianten und Stricharten.	Variantes et coups d'archet.	Variations and bowing-styles.
	Obměny a druhy smyků.	Варіанты и движенія смычка.

Ebenso die ganze Etude.
De même toute l'étude.
The same throughout the whole study.

Var. 1. Allegro. ♩ = 132

Var. 2. Allegro. ♪ = 152

) Alle mit M bezeichneten Stricharten in der Mitte, an der Spitze und am Frosch üben.	*) Travaillez les coups d'archet marqués de M* du milieu, de la pointe et du talon.	*) Practice each of the bowing-styles marked M* at the middle, the tip, and the frog.
	) Písmenem M označené smyky hrej středem, hrotem a u žabky.	*) Движенія смычка, обозначенныя M*. исполнять серединою, концомъ и у колодочки.

Copyright   by Bosworth & Co   B. & Cº 6127

4

Var. 3. Allegro.

Moderato.

Var. 4. Allegro.

Moderato.

Var. 5. Allegro.

Moderato.

Var. 6. Allegro.

Mit Stricharten 1-14 aus Var. 5. | Avec les coups d'archet 1-14 de la Var. 5. | With the bowing-styles shown in 1
Smyky 1-14 z variace páté. | to 14 of Variation 5.
Движеніями 1-14 изъ Var. 5.

Var. 7. Allegro.

Var. 8. Allegro. ♩ = 132   Var. 9. Allegro. ♩ = 132

Mit Stricharten 1-12 aus Var. 7. | Avec les coups d'archet 1-12 de la Var. 7. | With the bowing-styles shown in 1 to
                                 | *Smyky 1-12 z variace sedmé* | 12 of Variation 7.
                                 | | Движеніями 1-12 изъ Var. 7.

Var. 10. Allegro. ♪ = 152

Var. 11. Allegro. ♪ = 152

Mit Stricharten 1-14 aus Var. 10. | Avec les coups d'archet 1-14 de la Var. 10. | With the bowing-styles shown in 1 to
                                  | *Smyky 1-14 z variace desáté.* | 14 of Variation 10.
                                  | | Движеніями 1-14 изъ Var. 10.

Var. 12. Allegro. ♩ = 120

Var. 13. Allegro. ♩ = 120   Var. 14. Allegro. ♩ = 120

Mit Stricharten 1-6 aus Var. 12. | Avec les coups d'archet 1-6 de la Var. 12. | With the bowing-styles shown in 1 to
                                 | *Smyky 1-6 z variace čís. 12.* | 6 of Variation 12.
                                 | | Движеніями 1-6 изъ Var. 12.

Var. 15. Allegro. ♩ = 120

Var. 16. Allegro. ♩ = 120   Var. 17. Allegro. ♩ = 120

Mit Stricharten 1-6 aus Var. 15. | Avec les coups d'archet 1-6 de la Var. 15. | With the bowing-styles shown in 1 to
                                 | *Smyky 1-6 z variace č. 15.* | 6 of Variation 15.
                                 | | Движеніями 1-6 изъ Var. 15.

B. & Cº 6127

№ 32.

Arpeggien in Gruppen von 3 Noten mit 58 Veränderungen des Bogenstriches.	Arpèges en groupes de 3 notes avec 58 changements de coups d'archet.	Arpeggios in groups of 3 notes with 58 changes of bowing-styles.
	Arpežie ve skupinách o 3 notách s 58 změnami smyku.	Арпеджіи въ группахъ по 3 ноты съ 58 перемѣнами движенія смычка.

A) **Allegro moderato.**

B) **Allegro moderato.**

7

Stricharten.
Coups d'archet.
Bowing-styles.

Smyky.
Движенія см.

Moderato.

M Handgelenk.
Poignet.
Wrist.
Кистью.

Allegro.

spiccato

sautillé

B. & Cº 6127

№ 33.

Arpeggien in Gruppen von 4 Noten auf zwei Saiten. 3 Übungen mit 75 Veränderungen des Bogenstriches.

Arpèges en groupes de 4 notes sur deux cordes. 3 exemples avec 75 changements de coups d'archet.

Arpéžie ve skupinách o 4 notách na dvou strunách. 3 cvičení s 75 změnami smyku.

Arpeggios in groups of 4 notes on two strings. 3 examples with 75 changes of bowing-styles.

Арпеджіи въ группахъ по 4 ноты на двухъ струнахъ. 3 упражненія съ 75 перемѣнами движенія смычка.

Allegro moderato.

Daumenlage. | Position du pouce. / *Poloha palcová.* | Position of the Thumb. / Позиція большого пальца.

B.& Cᵒ 6127

Arpeggien in Octaven in der Dau-menlage.

Arpèges en octaves à la position du pouce.

Arpežie v oktávách polohy palcové.

Arpeggios in octaves in the Position of the Thumb.

Арпеджіи въ октавахъ въ позиціи большого пальца.

Stricharten.
Coups d'archet.
Bowing-styles.

Smyky.
Движенія см.

(Métr: ♩ = 100)

10

№ 34.

Arpeggien in Gruppen von 6 Noten mit 31 Veränderungen des Bogenstriches.

Arpèges en groupes de 6 notes avec 31 changements de coups d'archet.

Arpežie ve skupinách o 6 notách s 31 proměnami smyku.

Arpeggios in groups of 6 notes with 31 changes of bowing-styles.

Арпеджіи въ группахъ по 6 нотъ съ 31 перемѣною движенія смычка.

B.& Cᵒ 6127

№ 35.

Arpeggien in Gruppen von 8 Noton mit 23 Veränderungen des Bogenstriches

Arpèges en groupes de 8 notes avec 23 changements de coups d'archet.

Arpeggios in groups of 8 notes with 23 changes of bowing-styles.

Arpéžie ve skupinách o osminotách s 23 změnami smykovými.

Арпеджіи въ группахъ по 8 нотъ съ 23 перемѣнами движенія смычка.

Stricharten.
Coups d'archet.
Bowing-styles.

Smyky.
Движенія см.

№ 36.

Wechsel der Doppelgriffe mit einfachen Noten.
Zwei Beispiele mit 174 Varianten.

Changement de la double corde avec la simple.
Deux exemples avec 174 variantes.

Stŕídání dvojhmatů s notami jednoduchými.
Dva příklady s 174 variacemi.

Alternation of double-stoppings with single notes.
Two examples with 174 Variations.

Чередованіе двойныхъ съ простыми нотами.
Два примѣра съ 174 варіантами.

Veränderungen in Vierteln.

Variantes en noires.
Změny čtvrťové.

Variations in crotchets (quarter-notes).
Измѣненія четвертными.

Mit ganzcm Bogen.
Tout l'archet.
Whole bow-length.

Celým smyčcem.
Цѣлымъ смычкомъ.

Mit halbem Bogen.
Moitié de l'archet.
Half bow-length.

Polovici smyčce.
Половиною смычка.

Mit der Mitte.
Du milieu.
Bow-middle.

Středem.
Серединою.

B.& Cº 6127

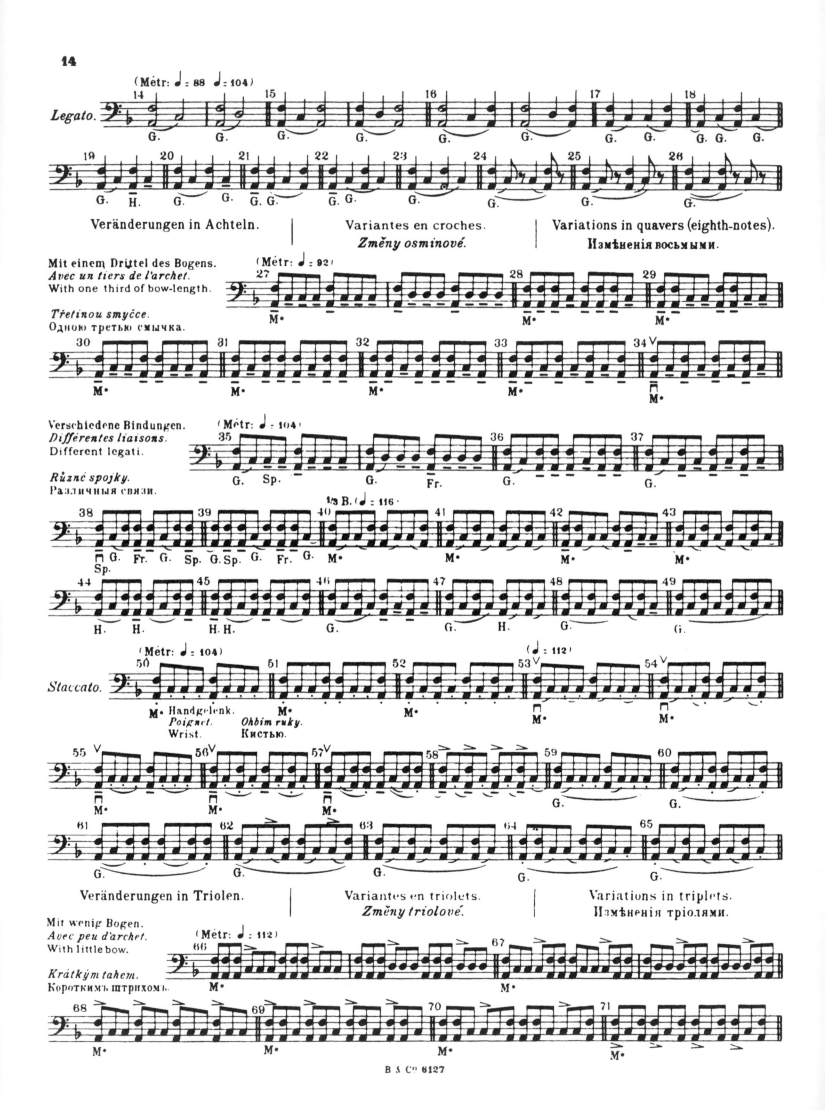

14

Legato.

Veränderungen in Achteln. | Variantes en croches. | Variations in quavers (eighth-notes).
Změny osminové. | Изменения восьмыми.

Mit einem Drittel des Bogens.
Avec un tiers de l'archet.
With one third of bow-length.

Třetinou smyčce.
Одною третью смычка.

Verschiedene Bindungen.
Différentes liaisons.
Different legati.

Různé spojky.
Различныя связи.

Staccato.

Handgelenk.
Poignet.
Wrist.
Ohbím ruky.
Кистью.

Veränderungen in Triolen. | Variantes en triolets. | Variations in triplets.
Změny triolové. | Изменения тріолями.

Mit wenig Bogen.
Avec peu d'archet.
With little bow.

Krátkým tahem.
Коротким штрихом.

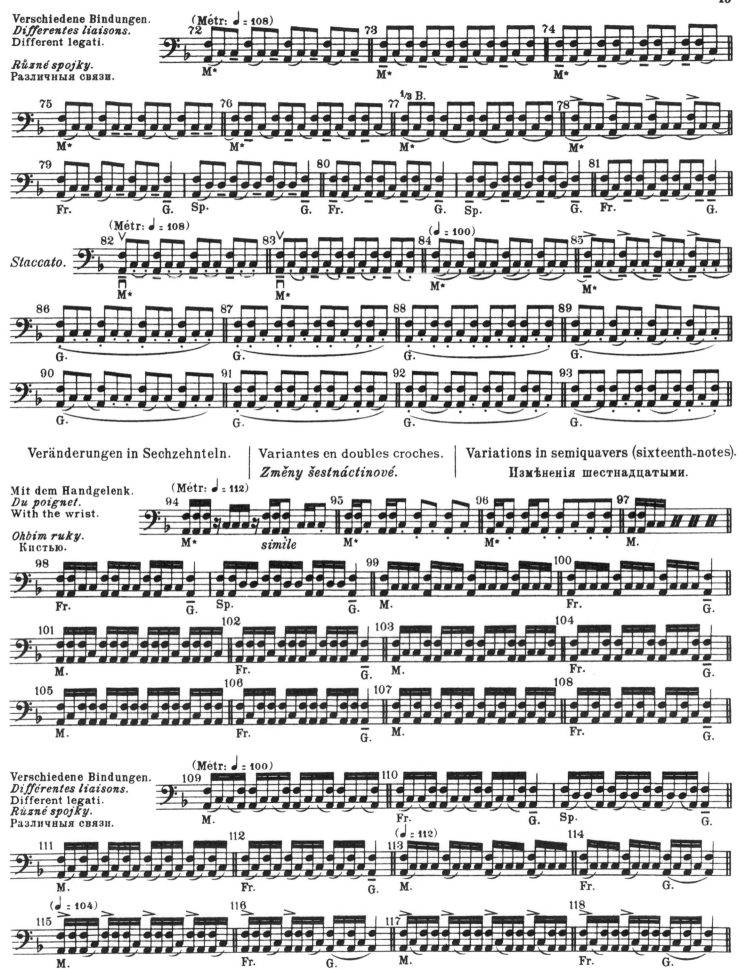